GHOST STORIES

GHOSTS IN PALACES

By Lisa Owings

EPIC

BELLWETHER MEDIA • MINNEAPOLIS, MN

EPIC BOOKS are no ordinary books. They burst with intense action, high-speed heroics, and shadows of the unknown. Are you ready for an Epic adventure?

This edition first published in 2017 by Bellwether Media, Inc.

No part of this publication may be reproduced in whole or in part without written permission of the publisher.
For information regarding permission, write to Bellwether Media, Inc., Attention: Permissions Department,
5357 Penn Avenue South, Minneapolis, MN 55419.

Library of Congress Cataloging-in-Publication Data

Names: Owings, Lisa, author.
Title: Ghosts in Palaces / by Lisa Owings.
Description: Minneapolis, MN : Bellwether Media Inc., 2017. | Series: Epic:
    Ghost Stories | Includes bibliographical references and index.
Identifiers: LCCN 2015047979 | ISBN 9781626174306 (hardcover : alk. paper)
Subjects: LCSH: Haunted palaces–Juvenile literature. | Haunted
    castles–Juvenile literature. | Ghosts–Juvenile literature.
Classification: LCC BF1474 .O95 2017 | DDC 133.1/22–dc23
LC record available at http://lccn.loc.gov/2015047979

TABLE OF CONTENTS

HAUNTED HALLS

You wander the halls of an old castle. Later, you see a shadow in your trip photos. Did someone, or something, else join you?

Palaces are full of mystery. Many have **cruel** pasts. Do suffering spirits haunt them?

THE BLOODY TOWER

Anne Boleyn became Queen of England in 1533. But she was soon **sentenced** to death. She was **accused** of **treason** and witchcraft.

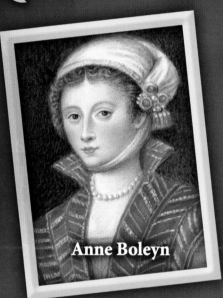

Anne Boleyn

England

N
W E
S

HISTORY CONNECTION

King Henry VIII was married when he met Anne. But divorce was unlawful for Catholics. He went against the Pope to make Anne queen.

Tower of London

The queen awaited death in the Tower of London. She was **beheaded** on May 19, 1536.

People see Anne's ghost throughout England. She often walks with her head tucked under her arm.

The Tower is one of Anne's favorite haunts. Her body was buried there.

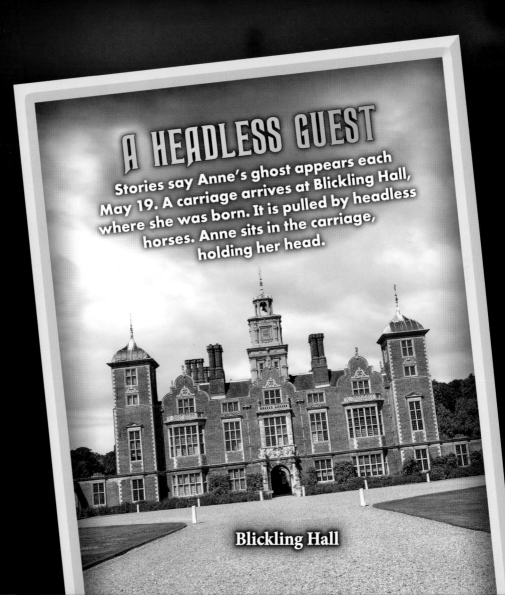

A HEADLESS GUEST

Stories say Anne's ghost appears each May 19. A carriage arrives at Blickling Hall, where she was born. It is pulled by headless horses. Anne sits in the carriage, holding her head.

Blickling Hall

One night, a guard saw a light in the Tower chapel. He climbed up to a window. Inside was a strange sight.

Ghostly figures in **ancient** clothing gathered there. One was a lovely woman. She looked exactly like paintings of Anne!

SIGHTINGS OF ANNE BOLEYN

- Guard stabs Anne's headless ghost and faints (1864)
- Guard sees a ghostly gathering led by Anne (late 1800s)
- Headless Anne arrives at Blickling Hall in a carriage drawn by headless horses (May 19 each year)
- Anne's ghost crosses drawbridge at her childhood home (December 24 each year)

GUARDING AGAINST GHOSTS

One guard met Anne's ghost and fainted. People thought he just fell asleep. But others had seen her ghost, too.

THE GHOST QUEEN

Elizabeth I was Anne Boleyn's daughter. She ruled England from 1558 until her death in 1603.

Elizabeth I

HISTORY CONNECTION

Queen Elizabeth I never married. She ruled well on her own. Her people loved her wit and charm.

Windsor Castle

It is said her ghost visits Windsor Castle. She appears most often in times of war.

Royal Library,
Windsor Castle

Elizabeth's ghost haunts the library at
Windsor. Her footsteps echo on the wood
floors. Then the grand queen appears,
wearing black.

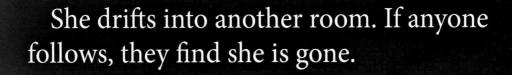

She drifts into another room. If anyone follows, they find she is gone.

DRESSED TO IMPRESS

Queen Elizabeth I cared about her royal image. She owned many fancy dresses and bright jewels.

King George III claimed to speak with the spirit. She called herself Elizabeth. She said she was married to England.
Could this famous queen be watching over her country, even in death?

King George III

SIGHTINGS OF QUEEN ELIZABETH I

- Speaks with King George III (late 1700s to early 1800s)

- Appears to King Edward VII (late 1800s to early 1900s)

- Visits King George VI several times (near World War II)

- Seen by Queen Elizabeth II and Princess Margaret

HAUNTINGS
OR
HEEBIE-JEEBIES?

Skeptics do not believe in palace hauntings. They say people hear ghost stories. Then their minds recreate them.

Some people think palaces are spooky. They are more likely to believe they see ghosts there.

One study suggests hauntings are real. A group of people walked through an English palace. They recorded strange events.

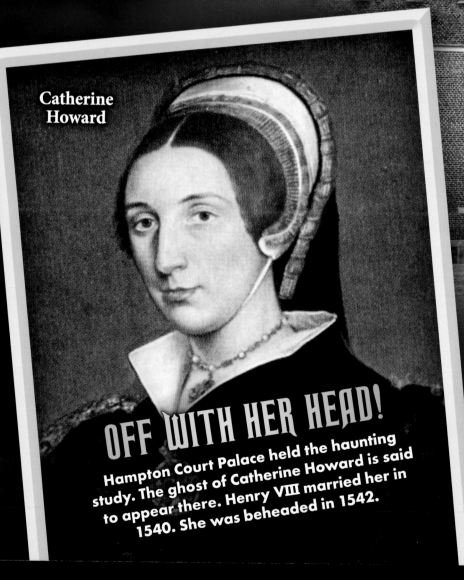

Catherine Howard

OFF WITH HER HEAD!

Hampton Court Palace held the haunting study. The ghost of Catherine Howard is said to appear there. Henry VIII married her in 1540. She was beheaded in 1542.

Most events happened in the same few rooms. Are these the chosen haunts of **royal** ghosts?

GLOSSARY

accused—said to have done something wrong

ancient—from long ago

beheaded—killed by having one's head cut off

cruel—causing harm or suffering

royal—related to kings and queens

sentenced—given a punishment by a court of law

skeptics—people who doubt the truth of something

treason—the crime of not being loyal to one's country

TO LEARN MORE

AT THE LIBRARY

Eding, June. *Who Was Queen Elizabeth?* New York, N.Y.: Grosset & Dunlap, 2008.

Higgins, Nadia. *Ghosts*. Minneapolis, Minn.: Bellwether Media, 2014.

Riley, Gail Blasser. *Tower of London: England's Ghostly Castle*. New York, N.Y.: Bearport Pub., 2007.

ON THE WEB

Learning more about ghosts in palaces is as easy as 1, 2, 3.

1. Go to www.factsurfer.com.

2. Enter "ghosts in palaces" into the search box.

3. Click the "Surf" button and you will see a list of related web sites.

With factsurfer.com, finding more information is just a click away.

INDEX